MW01593417

Concerti...
Psalms for the Pilgrimage

Poems by
Lynda Lambert

To Bob

Published by KotaPress
Vashon Island, WA
2002

ISBN 1-929359-18-7
Library of Congress Control Number: 2002112554

Copyrights
2002 Poetry & Original Art by Lynda Lambert
2002 Cover & Layout Design by KotaPress

Publisher
KotaPress
Vashon Island, WA
info@kotapress.com
www.KotaPress.com

See Colophon for acknowledgement of special
individual supporters.

Table of Contents

Table of Contents Con't...

Table of Contents Con't...

Foreword

Light falling on Alpine villages, a stone street in Berchtesgaden, the memorial at Lidice (where 88 children were among the 483 slaughtered of this Czech village), jagged mountains wrapped in mist, a Picasso or Miro' hanging in a museum, the centuries-old domed cathedral of Salzburg, fields blooming with Queen Anne's lace -- these are among Lynda Lambert's subjects in her first book of poems. Each poem is a tribute to the thing itself, caught in a moment of time and introspection blended with her artist's eye for color, light, texture (the heft of a pink stone in the palm of her hand), and tone. Moreover, each poem is itself a chord of memory with a place in the whole, for this work comprises a journey of an artistic sensibility moving between awe, fear and joy -- all woven by the sophisticated interplay of word and sound through the alembic of memory. Lambert is part Dickinson (the later and better E.D.) in her love of natural beauty for the sheer physicalness of things seen in nature. But even more so, she reminds one of Rilke, that most original and modern of European poets, the Prague-born poet of Austria, whose rarefied practice of seeing the object and lifting it to a contemplation of its essence to expose its inner core is so original that it cannot be paraphrased.

Although her poems follow a three-part (past, present, and future) interlocking that binds the whole, her style varies interestingly and adroitly throughout each section -- for example, many later poems have a concrete simplicity, such as "Königsee" and "Grödig Stone," and the moodier poems of the present section with their longer lines and varied rhythms might be followed by a playful "found" poem like "Traveling

Song" or an experimental form like "Memorial Day - a Sestina for Multiple Voices," which latter poem exists easily alongside the spare "Slowly, Suddenly" in the final segment. The circular, rather than the linear, without a terminus to the journey, is no doubt a deliberate aspect of her design for the whole.

"May I serve you?" her narrative voice asks of the reader in both line and title with beguiling simplicity, at once offering art's nourishment to the spirit as well as expressing its enduring humility in service to humanity. Everywhere Lambert acknowledges the demands made on the artist's own psyche through interminable periods of drought or, as she says in "Mandate," in "sweat and waiting." Best of all, I believe, we readers acclimate easily to her struggle and her own humility as she finds her voice in the common theme of aspiring to create art from this striving against her emotions and her self-as-artist. The struggle to use these words so that the poems become compositions as integral to her journey of discovery as her many sketches, journal entries, photographs and mixed-media compositions interspersed throughout the book is a rewarding journey for the reader. The artists to whom she pays an occasional homage - Picasso, Ernst, Klee, Miro' - are all a part of her own attempt to use the rhythms of words to shape the thoughts that make this first collection a delight for the mind as well as the senses.

-Terry White
John Steinbeck,
The Good Companion, 2002

Part I

Past...Marks gouged in sand and stone

...all past events are more remote from our senses than the stars of the remotest galaxies, whose own light at least still reaches the telescopes. But the moment just past is extinguished forever, save for the things made during it.

George Kubler

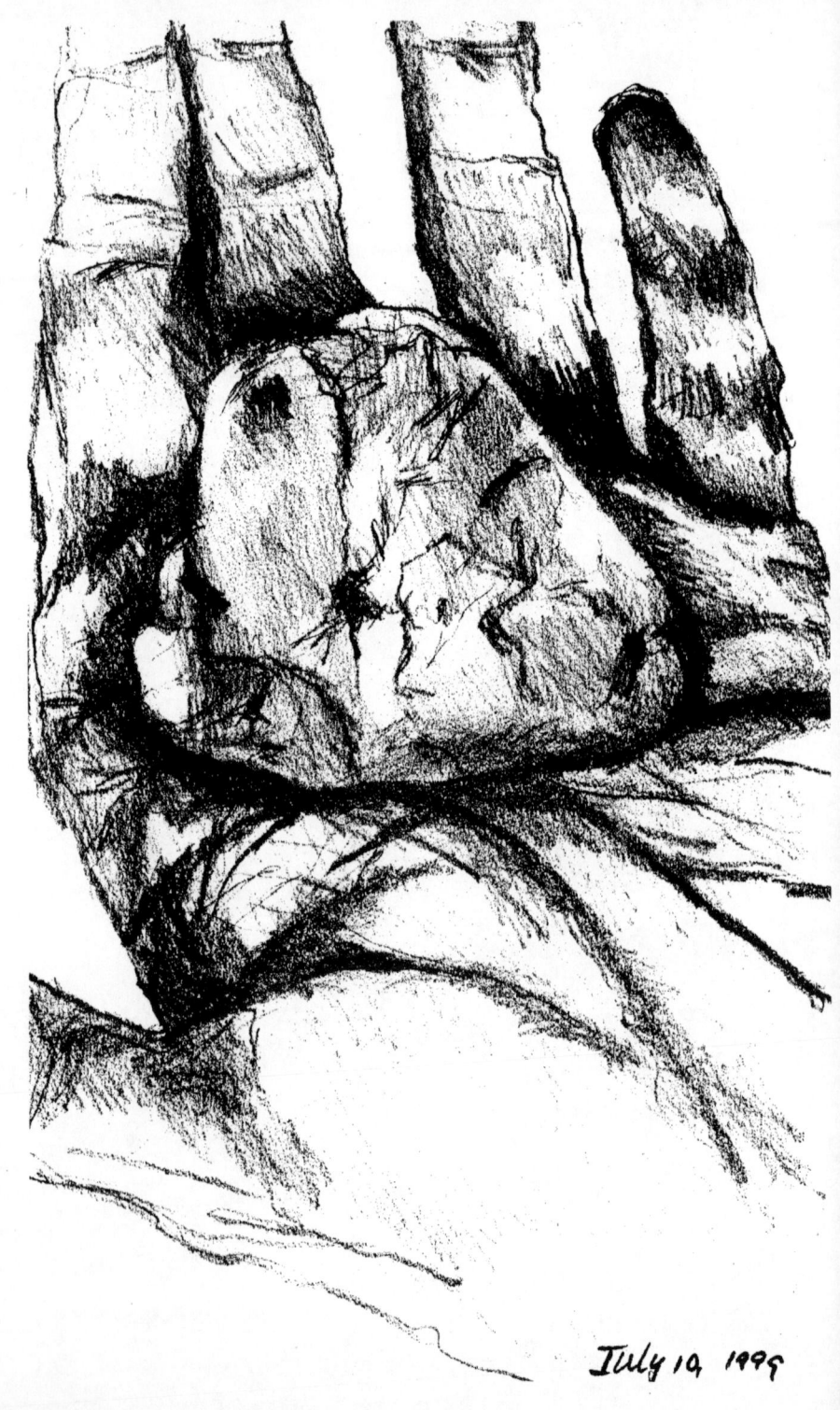

July 19 1999

A Memory Within a Memory

The unfolding
of a story-
marks
gouged in sand and stone
washed up on barren beaches
reaching upward
across time
and scattered
among
rumors.

(Reflecting on *Et in Arcadia Ego* by Nicholas Poussin)

Requiem Mass

In the darkness of winter
the city
lays in a crescent
beneath my window
I seem to remember
lonely sounds
a Requiem Mass.

In the brightness of summer
the city
moves like a symphony
surrounds me
I clearly remember
sorrow sounds
a Requiem Mass.

What goes around
does not
come back around.

Historical Note:

The earliest records concerning the village of Lidice can be found in the 13th century. The village was dominated by St. Martin's church. It was a typical Czech village and had the first school with central heating in Bohemia in the 1700's.

St Martin's church was destroyed during the Hussite wars and again in the Thirty Years' war. It was rebuilt and decorated by Czech artists.

On June 9, 1942 the village of Lidice had 102 houses and 493 residents. The oldest woman was 88 years. The youngest infant was 2 weeks. There were 14 farms and a mill in the village.

On June 10, the shooting began:

192	men shot dead
7	women shot dead
52	women martyred in the concentration camp
88	children assassinated

The entire village of Lidice was leveled to the ground.

Book of Remembrance in Lidice

In the museum
a Book of Remembrance
records the facts -
names, dates, village

A Plexiglas box
holds debris -
sand and dirt
human remains

A basket of flowers on
an embroidered hanky
with lace around the edges
hands clasped in friendship
on a corner of the lace scallop.

Envelopes
with tea colored letters
faded red stamps
written in pencil
postmarked.

A wall for men
A wall for women
with photos and
names
of the dead
posted.

Eighty-two bronze children stand
In the field just off the path
It's a secluded place
beneath a solitary pine tree
where chicory frolics with the grass.

I imagine it was such a lovely summer meadow
Clover, Sweet Peas, Dandelion,
Crown Vetch, Queen Anne's Lace
a large snail in a smooth spiral shell
beneath the silent pine tree.

Zum Gedenhen an die millionen kinder, Die Dem 11.
Weltkrieg zum opfer gefallen sind.

In Memoriam – Jahre 1942
The Children of Lidice

A Sestina for Alfred Rieder's Widow

Alfred Rieder's widow arrives early this morning.
She stands awhile among the fading ribbons
then bends low to light a candle near the edge of the wilting flowers.
The churchyard is alive with the movement and scent of summer
and a wooden cross at the top of Alfred Rieder's grave stands swaged in black lace.
Two others embrace this new widow.

The three speak softly, voices hushed near the edge of the path.
They never turn around to that I have come here this morning.
Both women, in mourning black, reach out and rearrange the limp ribbons,
admire the many large bouquets of flowers.
The only fresh ones are the yellow centered daises this summer
with a golden message, "**Dia**," written on the white streamer of lace.

A quiet breeze comes to lift the edges of black lace
attached to the top of the cross where three stand on the path.
The bell in the church tower strikes eleven times this morning.
They never notice the brilliant foil letters on the pale violet ribbons
or the small bee that moves quickly among the pastel flowers
continuing to stop and taste the sweet blossoms of summer

or the strong-winged butterfly that moves through the graveyard this summer
and no interest in the marble stones, or the cross, or the flapping lace.
It finds fresher flowers blooming further down the winding path.
Alfred Rieder's grave overflows with messages of love this morning.
The three sigh as they read aloud from the gilded ribbons
woven through spikes of lavender larkspur, ferns, and pink flowers.

There are pinecone wreaths, rosettes and small bouquets of flowers
too many to fit on the space of his fresh new grave this summer.
The sun and rains will slowly dissolve flowers and lace
that overflow from the gravesite onto the garden path.
This year Alfred Rieder's widow will visit his grave each morning
bring little bouquets, cut flowers tied with satin ribbons.

12

She will grow older, cry less often, and neglect the fancy ribbons.
She'll come here summer evenings to water the flowers
she'll bring freshly cut flowers from her garden each summer.
In the fall she will offer bronze mums tied with golden lace.
Her sturdy black shoes will walk firmly on the autumn path
as she nods a silent greeting to another new widow one morning.

The new widow stands knee-deep in ribbons, flowers, and lace.
On another summer day the hot sun wilts fragile flowers
Alfred Rieder's widow walks down the path to console a friend this morning.

Note: Written in Grödig, Austria at the church graveyard, July, 1998

13

Holy Mary Mother of God

When I saw you last
you were dressed in beaten gold
bronze stars encircled your head
your bare feet balanced on a sharp
crescent moon

I was forced to lift my eyes
towards heaven
because you watched me
light the votive candle
and linger awhile
in your presence.

Our Lady, we will meet again
Please remember me.

Journal Entry at Alfred Rieder's Grave, 2000

A green watering can peeks from behind the left side of the upright tombstone. Its black plastic spout extends outward as though reaching towards the lush green ivy covered fence just behind the row of gravesites.

Today's bouquet is fresh – sherbet orange lilies with cinnamon pistils – wide open to expose the center from which each petal and stamen flows from the single flower. It opens to face towards the stone on which is carved:

HEIR RUHTIN FRIEDEN
ALFRED RIEDER
5.9.1929 + 8.7.1998

Alfred Rieder's photo is set into his gravestone now. He is dressed in a suit, wears a tie. He looks directly at me. He is so handsome. It appears as if he is about to be going to take care of business today with his face frozen in the moment between a smile and a question. His eyes are strong, and he looks up to recognize my presence this morning as the sun warms my hand on the page.

The Berchtesgadener Street Stone

Cool rain falls, a transparent veil
beyond this Alpine village, mist covers the mountain
Holding a pink stone in my left hand
I watch from behind a glass door.

Beyond this Alpine Village, mist covers the mountain
I remember walking to St. Leonhardt one morning
I watch from behind a glass door
I have become the mother of the earth.

As I remember walking to St. Leonhardt one morning
wide fields of Queen Anne's lace, full bloom
I have become the mother of the earth
A small pink stone nestled in the sand near my feet.

Wide fields of Queen Anne's lace, full bloom
at the base of the mountain on Berchtesgadener Street
A small pink stone, nestled in the sand near my feet
half buried in sand and soft damp earth.

At the base of the mountain on Berchtesgadener Street
I bent down to lift the stone from the field
half buried in sand and soft damp earth
held it and walked till the winds wiped it dry.

I bent down to lift the stone from the field
we walked home together, the stone and I
held it and walked till the winds wiped it dry
a triangle shaped lump with rounded corners.

We walked home together, the stone and I
soft pink marble mingled with gray
a triangle shaped lump with rounded corners
rose-colored veins lie just below the skin.

16

Soft pink marble mingled with gray
beneath a translucent surface
rose-colored veins lie just below the skin
cuts and scars from a life that's been harsh.

Beneath a transparent surface
a scarred pink stone speaks of a long journey
cuts and scars from a life that's been harsh
a cool stone warms in the palm of my hand.

A scarred pink stone speaks of a long journey
as rain pours from the dense fog in the sky
a cool stone warms in the palm of my hand
as I watch the mountain mingle with mist.

As rain pours from the dense fog in the sky
the stone brings life to my body
as I watch the mountains mingle with mist
its rained every day since I arrived.

The stone brings life to my body
jagged mountain edges emerge in the distance
its rained every day since I arrived
mist, clouds, and sky conspire to make mountains vanish.

Jagged mountain edges emerge in the distance
the ultimate magic show takes place
mist, clouds, and sky conspire to make mountains vanish
I shift in my seat and listen to cars moving outside.

The ultimate magic show takes place
the stone turns over in my hand
I shift in my seat as cars move outside
one warm thing on a cold rainy morning.

The stone turns over in my hand
it throbs and moves, warmer than my body
one warm thing on a cold rainy morning
the Berchtesgadener Street Stone clutched in my hand.

A Mandate

Enter deeply into this wood
chisel, rip, cut, and tear
until you reveal
the images that are
locked within.

There is life inside
slabs of dead wood.
no one will ever know
about this world
until the surface
is torn away.

Art is made
from created things -
solid rock, faith in God,
dirt of the earth,
fire and water,
sweat and waiting.

Journal Entry
July 8, 1999

We hold up our umbrellas and weep together for joy in
the presence of Austria. Have we come home at last?

I begin to draw once again. Draw for my life.
Draw to create a memory to stay with me when long
winter days try to make me forget summer and Austria.

But for now, begin to make a list – things that will be
the beginnings of a poem – many poems.

We remember today that we have lost our fathers and
the orange fields remind us of our loss. I will return
alone after dark and close the rose curtains.

20

A Song of Austria

Can you sing for me a song of Austria?
Sing about papal treasures
and jewels in the golden monstranz
inside Salzburg Cathedral.

Let me hear the sounds
of the bombs that dropped
and fires that blazed
when the buildings were destroyed.

Take me on ancient paths
where Celts and Romans used to walk.
Let me see signs and wonders along the way
and taste salt inside the mountain.

Can you sing about golden angels
carved in the wooden altars?
or goats on the Alpine hills?
or teams of horses that pull the wagons?

I desire to listen to the waters of Mondsee
draw the sailboats on the lake
and the silence of the absent souls
that rises from ancient bones in Halstatt.

I will lay back my head and look at the mountain tops
as you sing of distant roads
that meander through the lush green hills
as we turn to begin the long ride home.

Dom zu Salzburg

Ecclesiastical architecture
papal treasures
Salzburg's Cathedral
constructed by Virgil
the facade records 744

Consecration by fire 1628
holy treasures
destroyed
Romanesque Cathedral
rebuilt by two archbishops.

Inauguration by bombs
damaged by a world at war
rebuilt 1959
conserved Cathedral
a treasure in the south.

Concert in the Fortress

Red fluted pillars
black ruffles on a swinging skirt
golden metal stars.

Flags of red and white
bouquets of flowers and music
arches frame night skies.

Stone paths, shields, blazons
singing and chess in the town square
Salzburg in July.

*(Note: Construction on the Hohensalzburg was begun
in the year 1077. The Golden Hall was added in 1502.
Concerts are held here under the blue ceiling with the
gold leafed buttons symbolizing the stars in heaven.
Four spiral columns of red marble support the ceiling.)*

Christmas Angel

Surrounded by her family
an aged queen
slowly
opens gifts

memories of winter grass
float amid waters
dormant
inside airless bottles

She forgets about
the next snowfall.

Surrounded

Problems far too big for me to solve
are piled higher than my head. -Psalms 40:12

The image - me - in the center
Surrounded with problems - sins
They are stacked - high
Higher than my head - heaps
Piled so high they tower above me - surrounded
Problems - sins
I am in darkness as they merge
Outside light is shut out
No view of anything - alone
Isolated from all sources of help - unseen
In a cavern of isolation - unknown
I am hidden deeply inside the ring
Accumulation of problems - sin

Only you Lord can hear my heart - beating
I stand in fear - near death
Only you Lord can see my head bent - shame
I stand in shame - without you
In airless space - without light
I am feeble - shaking
I cry out to you.

Come now - rescue
Lift me from this place
See me here - lonely
Ashamed
You are my only hope - Higher
Lift me higher
I know you will.

Historical Note:

Mirabell Palace, originally called Altenau, was built in 1606 by the Prince-Archbishop Wolf Dietrich von Raitenau as a home for his mistress Salome Alt and their children. The famous Mirabell Gardens surround the palace. They were designed by Fischer von Erlach. On the grounds are stone unicorns, a Pegasus fountain, gloriously blooming flowers spilling from large urns and a magical rose garden all enclosed by local wrought ironwork.

Wolfe spent the final six years of his life imprisoned in Hohensalzburg Fortress that overlooks the city of Salzburg. The fortress was his destiny as he was held prisoner until his death in 1612.

I have imagined Wolfe may have smuggled love notes to Salome during those six years of imprisonment.

Salome's Garden -
Love Notes From Wolfe, Smuggled From Prison

I
If we could have measured
the length of our time on earth
before we began the journey
I would have hoped
for golden days
alone, in the garden
with you.

II
Does Pegasus fly
when waxed begonias bloom in
Mirabell's Garden?

III
Is our garden lush
yellow marigolds touched by
morning's cool damp mist?

IV
Do our marble stairs
come to life during the night
when the putti dance?

V
The orangery waits
near the end of the garden
hidden, out of view.

VI
The scent of roses
permeated my cell tonight
just before twilight.

VII
Salome and Wolfe
we danced down pink marble stairs
hot candles flickered.

VIII
Lions guard our steps
to the secret garden path
where the dwarfs carouse.

IX
Raphael Donner
created putti to frolic
on pink marble crests.

X
I miss your soft touch
long to be near you at the
end of my journey.

XI
You are my crown jewel
in the snow that melts away
everything I touch.

XII
When our garden fades
icy frost covers windows
I will remember you.

XIII
Our children will dance
in gardens we created from
Imagination.

July 16, 19 91

Part II

Present...Reaching upward across time

I notice that as I live from day to day, observing and feeling what goes on both inside and outside myself, certain aspects of what is happening adhere to me, as if magnetized by a center of psychic gravity. I have learned to trust this center, to rely on its acuity and to go along with its choices although the center itself remains mysterious to me. I sometimes feel as if I recognize my own experience. It is a feeling akin to that of unexpectedly meeting a friend in a strange place, of being at once startled and satisfied – startled to find outside myself what feels native to me, satisfied to be so met. It is exhilarating.

Anne Truit

July 6, 1991

Venezia, 7 a.m.

I hear deep bell sounds
from the Renaissance tower
morning announcements
arrive in waves
embrace me low
surround me deep.

A duet begins
to shape this early light
mingled with lapping
pushing
surging
waves in the lagoon.

Polished black boats are tied
to terra cotta stone piers
covered by slippery gray mists

An unrelenting shrill voice
somewhere
out of view
soars over
aqua cleansing waters.

Four Chinese women pause
form a circle
their heads lean back
mouths open wide as they laugh
at fat pigeons taking staccato strides

The thin man in green cotton pants nods
as he sweeps away the debris
from the all-night celebration
his long flexible broom
scrapes away trash and fireworks
scattering them into the heavens.

The scratching of his broom
mingles with the chorus
of bells, birds, water,
women's chatter
and the movement of my hand
as I write in this journal.

It is the morning after
Redentore Festival
once again
the Redeemer's fireworks
have saved us from the plague.

It has now been 400 years
his sparks have kept us safe.

Bon Giorno!
Bon Giorno!

34

Fragments

Alone in the
middle of the night
I gather fragments -
number them,
listen
to them,
look for a seed
that could become
a new poem.

Go over them
once again
in the morning
and try
to remember them.

Tonight I needed
to write a poem.

Domplatz

A fortress broods above the city
dark against the afternoon sky
courtyard walls surround me.

Behind a monument to my right
a pigeon briefly appears
then swiftly flies through the Roman arch.

There are words of wisdom and songs
as evening begins to descend
the heavy fortress grows a darker gray.

The Austrian driver wears a pointed hat
leans back and rounds the corner
two bells sound from twin towers.

At 6:30 I am alone
carts continue to pass below
no one hurries here tonight

Two boys have stopped to play
red and green balloons rise towards the towers
as I walk back to the bus stop.

The woman with a feather in her hat
sings from the square
beyond my view.

Resolved
Re: solved

Afternoon flickers
tiny lights on deep pine
snow comes tonight in Atlanta
grandfather sleeps
to deep music

Resolved
Re: solved

A cold fireplace
the dog sleeps
hind leg held high
in the air

Resolutions
Re: solutions

Figures from storybooks
advent passes
father works tonight
mother sleeps
in the large room

Repressed
Re: pressed

Figures emerge from paintings
above the fireplace
my mouth fills with coarse hairs
never completely removed
darkness in the thick paint

Retro: right to left

Eyes swollen, marching
no sleep this night
new toys, soft voices
swollen stories
new snow drifts
a checkbook out of balance

Revisit
Re: visit

I could make - - - a rainbow outside
I could be - - - ready to go
I could - - - a rainbow inside
Get a spoon and roll it!

Hold the plastic figure   Retail
dreaming upstairs   Re: tale
unprepared, falling apart
how many voices should

                                      Tell my story?

I've been waiting for you
I will use what you have
to tell my story.

A Side Trip

The destination today
salt mine at Berchtesgarten
taste the vitality of the salt
coveted by Celts, Romans,
Germanic tribes   Schellenberg
Sample the salt   Zimmer fri
Watch the signs along the way
Dip your fingers into the brine
Taste the salt
and want more!

Little dwarves painted into stucco
sing from houses
along the way.

Bavaria
Hallein
St. Wolfgangsee
Halstatt
Mondsee

Michael Pachel carved dark wood
into a golden altarpiece for devotion
a place for an angel gilded with gold.

I run up the hillside
to greet old friends
goats want to be touched
with satisfaction in my hand

The cart is pulled down the street
by two strong horses
chestnut bodies ripple
tan manes brushed to the side
loden green lone driver
eight passengers face each other
laughing in the narrow streets

Later, the blonde woman
will search for mountain hiking hats
in the small alpine shops

Here in St. Wolfgangsee
I have found the plate
with strokes that please me

I hand it over
to be wrapped for the journey home.

After an All-night Rain
(Remembering Dante)

Do not forget to mark my passage
Watch as I move through tall grass and honeysuckle vines
Breathe, breathe as you pass through the woods.

Feel the air that thickens with heavy rains
Squat low, search for broad plants under sheltering trees
Do not forget to mark my passage.

Reach out, mingle the poison ivy vines
with strong-scented honeysuckle tangles
Breathe, breathe as you pass through the woods.

Trace the withering crimson tips of white flowers
on the hardened muddy knoll
Do not forget to mark my passage.

Move your feet quietly this morning
past the sleeping dogs on the hillside
Breathe, breathe as you pass through the woods.

Listen as a small dog barks twice
in the darkened room where my mother sleeps
Do not forget to mark my passage.
Breathe, breathe as you pass through the woods.

Historical Note:

Halstatt, a village in central Austria became a site whose name was used to denote the Early (800-500 BC) and Late (500 BC-AD200) Iron Ages. The site flourished between the 7th and 5th centuries because of the salt mines.

Halstatt was a melting pot for influences from all sides of the Alps. Two thousand graves have been excavated in Halstatt's astonishing early Celtic cemetery.

The Halstattian's, like the Greeks, observed the symposium. It was a banquet at which the faithful companions of the deceased assembled for the final time. Many locally made bronze vessels have been found at gravesites in Halstatt.

The village was completely isolated in the heart of the Salzkammergut region and is accessible only by river. (Eluere) Today, there is one way into the village through a dark, winding mountain tunnel.

Halstatt

At the end of a narrow mountain road
winding down to the bottom
nestled among the rocks and trees -
Return.

I walked this rain soaked pathway
entered the house of bones
where skulls are on display -
Eternity.

There is a castle just across the lake
concealed from our view for awhile
we slowly approach that shore -
Distance.

Our boat touches the sun-tipped surface of rain
We watch a red train
passing through the mountain trail -
Halstatt.

Monday Afternoon Dessert with Friends

On Monday
afternoon
the friends
arrived
with gifts
concealed
in canvas bags.

We talked about
poetry and
inspiration
and dreamed about
trips to Europe,
and writing down
the words.

I unwrapped
the ivy vase
and wore
a golden pen
my fingers were
painted with silver
as I touched the book
of drawings.

In celebration of the Poetry Ladies Group -
In honor of Jean Cooper; in Memory of June
Kerstetter and Ida Barton.

44

This is I TODAY

This is I who splashed my body
with a cool blue perfume
put on a backpack loaded
with maps and a bus pass
to begin a day of travel.

This is I who climbed steep
ancient stone steps
paused at the top of a mountain
to share my special place
with friends as we looked out
over the city.

This is I who saw a homeless man
asleep behind a locked iron gate
beneath a camaflogue blanket
in a space that was made for Jesus.

This is I who watched people
climbing and descending the stairs
some stopped to take a look
at the drawing in my book.

This is I walking down Steingasse
beginning to weave the fiber
of a new dream
that is lingering in my mind.

This is I eating lunch
under the yellow umbrella
talking about brown butter,
Austrian noodles, mineral water and cold Coke.
Counting a stack of shillings
to pay for my meal.

This is I shopping on Linzer Gasse
buying German hand creme and toothpaste
wooden crayons and books
a new pair of Austrian shoes.

This is I writing letters to my mother and sister
while I sit in the shade
Mirabell garden
I wrote of my life today
and desired to share afternoon sun.

This is I remembering yesterday
watching parachutes and black birds
flying over the mountain
and a little blue flower
picked by a friend.

This is I who wonders
if the new dream can ever become real
a studio and time to paint
illusions, impressions
of my soft spoken desires.

For Delaunay Elise

We celebrate this Sabbath with
a birth on Sunday morning.

You awaken to this world
with lusty screams.

We stand and listen
awaiting the word.

Your Grandmother comes
to say
"It's a girl!"

Your first photo-
a white eyelet dress,
lavender satin ribbons
and a white lace
halo to surround your head.

We touch your
soft fingers
and kiss your closed eyes.

You dream.

A Drawing for Delaunay Elise

My arms know how
to gather completeness
and gently encircle
your delicate form.

I have strength
enough for the moment
for you are fragile
and changing inside.

I remain constant
and begin to draw.

Lookin' Good

I felt so good today
Shimmering
All day long
I'm a changed woman
Dressed in black
California stretch jersey
Bangles on the collar
Black high heels
Black pantyhose
Black leather mini-skirt
Slim and tiny
That's what I'm becoming
My life is changing
In Neiman-Marcus style.

Step right up. The world is waiting.

Two Friends on a Bench

Two friends on a bench
Comfort each other
Relaxed conversation

A scratch of the head
A nod, touch of the arm
A gesture of the hand, a look

The afternoon passes
two pigeons fly
under the bench

Old friends never notice
the people walking by
they only see each other

From a hidden tree branch
a bird begins to sing
love songs for them.

Dreams

Is there a way
I could bring back
dreams -
to examine them
like a work of art?

Could I create
something that would
last -
would I remember
it in the morning?

A Dream of Drawing in the Dark

When drawing in the dark
visions and forms appear
then vanish quickly
moving across
the inner vision —
of my night sky.

A panoramic vision
ever changing
highly charged
molten lava
when I draw in the dark
in the middle of the night.

Art Underground

I've been
working
on a plan
to put
art
back into
life.

The plan
was to
include
a gallery
yet,
when I
looked
all I could see
was
lots of rooms
for musicians
and a
very big stage.
I will
continue
to make pictures
in the
basement.

May I Serve You?

Here are the stacks of paintings
for you to look at tonight.
I have carefully brought them out
of storage closets
arranged them here
in the kitchen -
where my children used to play
games around a square table.

Once, food to nourish the body was
prepared here, by my hands.
Tonight, there is an
abundance of food
for your soul.

Come into my kitchen
and taste the world,
prepared by my hands.

A Winter Dream in Green

What is it
you see here?
Tell me
what should
I see?

It is green,
green and green -
sunlight on ice
filled with flesh
beneath

A round sun
bold, yellow
flowing waters
moving
rushing.

Swept away -
Can you
greens of summer
daybreak
in winter?

Dragon Fly

Winter dreams
come to us in color -
red-violet
blue-green
gold.

Memories merge
with the ice
and the heat
of the cool
winter sun.

We drift along
in the stream
awake and alive
only to learn
that we can fly.

We lived a life
below the water's surface
not knowing when
we would emerge,
for a brief
flight
before we die.

Another Dream

Dreaming with my eyes closed
alert to sounds around me -
I wonder about the difference
awake or asleep
and how can I know
which one is now?

Paintings are born
when the dreamer
reports to work
on time.

Flotsam, Jetsam, and the River - Homage to Biko

Wood fragments gathered at the river's edge
engorged between steel hull and muddy shore
from the bridge above, I could see them wedged
shifting on lapping waves, aft and fore.

Engorged between steel hull and muddy shore
waters glistened like strings of jet beads
shifting on lapping waves, aft and fore
broken, falling, shifting, wind-blown seeds.

Waters glistened like strings of jet beads
as the Dark Shaman weaves thick steel rings
broken, falling, shifting, wind-blown seeds
he weaves a memory world as he sings.

Of wood fragments at the river's edge
from the bridge above, I could see them wedged.

Post Cards From Prague

I
Sapphire light mingles with deep red violet
Rolled out behind the spiky black twin spires
Like a futuristic vision.
My neck aches from bending backwards
My soul leaps forward to embrace them.
Evening comes to Prague
Like a dark, warm wool blanket
That wraps a weary traveler's body
At the end of a long journey.

II
Tonight, walking along hard stone paths
The dark Moldau sang to me.
Her voice lifted me up from the street
Like a duet of a finely tuned violin
And a velvet throated cello
As we crossed the wide bridge
Keeping inside the dark shadows.
I watched a long gray pigeon
Quietly fly through the last ray of light
Coming home for rest
We continued searching
For the way back
To where the night begins.

III
Here in Prague
Store windows dazzle
With ample treasures of amber,
Garnets and Bohemian glass.
They bulge with heavy burdens of color
And ask me to return again tomorrow.
Come. Walk inside of me.

Touch. Hold. Buy.
I ask "what is the price?"
How will I carry the large glass flowers home?
How will they look when I place them
In a thick orange vase
From West Virginia?

IV
At the Pyramida Hotel
A small ink drawing hangs
On the wall in room 428.
This familiar artist's style
Catches my eye again.
His drawings hang
In my Pennsylvania home.

Last year, in Prague
The artist stood alone
Displaying his drawings
On Sunday morning.
A proud businessman.
I bought several.
The price was too low.

V
I sit alone
On the edge of the spiral tide
In the center of this night
My thoughts turn like a labyrinth
Made of ocean waves.
Soon you will embrace me
And we will walk away together.

VI
One by one
He looked at each passport
He wears two stars on each shoulder
An Eight-pointed star on his chest
A gun on his right hip.
Foolish students giggle in the back of the bus
One asks if he speaks English
He asks if they speak Czech
All laugh at his joke
He is thin and young
And departs with an English "Good Bye."
We occupied seven minutes of his day.

VII
It rains now
as we get our final glimpse of Prague
the translucent gray sky
softens the deep golden fields to mauve
distant trees turn from yellow-green
to blue wine mist.

VIII
Prostitutes take their places
along the road to Prague
they kneel down on the grass
squat low
wave at the tourists
bend forward
arrange their few possessions
in a small backpack.

IX
The late summer rains
have swept away
all our dreams.

Notes from the Baroque Museum
July 21, 1999

Antonio Pellegrini (1675-1741)

The format of this picture is a square with corners painted brown. This leaves an undulating cross shape in the center where the action of the painting takes place.

There is a rather narrow gold frame and the inside edges are fluted like gentle waves all around the picture's edges.

Two white horses criss-cross. One flies over and behind the other. Two other horses, one tan and one brown, plunge towards the bottom left corner.

It is only now I realize the four horses were pulling a chariot and there has been an accident!

The chariot has overturned and the charioteer falls toward the bottom right corner – his bent leg indicates he will not fall freely through the sky. His body will be stopped as he is caught on the chariot.

A being with wings hovers above the chaos – like a large gray goose. On the back of the goose rides a white bearded man. His right arm is high above his head and he leans toward the chariot wreck. The actions all take place in the heavens amid pink and tan clouds that float in a diagonal from the bottom left to the top right. The sky is a heavy cobalt blue and it thrusts the white horses forward towards me.

There seems to be a fire in the sky, which sears the mane of the brown horse as he falls toward me and I stand here watching the sky and the fire, and the events that are taking place.

I am helpless.

View from mirabell Gardens
7-13-91   Sunday 10-11 AM

Part III

Future...Scattered among rumors

As often happens on the spiritual journey, we have arrived at the heart of a paradox: each time a door closes, the rest of the world opens up. All we need to do is stop pounding on the door that just closed, turn around—which puts the door behind us—and welcome the largeness of life that now lies open to our souls. The door that closed kept us from entering a room, but what now lies before us is the rest of reality.

Parker Palmer

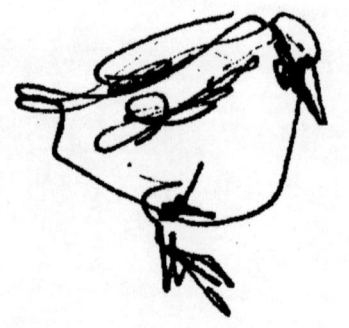

A Finely Crafted Traveling Song for the New Year

Rushing towards Charlotte
North on I-85
Around noon

FIREWORKS   PEACHES   CONTINENTAL BREAKFAST

Coca-Cola truck
Faded red signs   SEASON'S GREETINGS
Clemson fans moving South
towards the Peach Bowl
Flags, Tiger Paws   Black and Orange
Good Times in the Country

PEACHES   NECTARINES   APPLES
along the way
Crossing Buffalo Creek
PEACHES   We grow our own
The Sweetest Around

200 miles north of Atlanta
A Giant Peach
30 - 70% Savings
Gaffney Water Tower   THIS EXIT

An Eagle advertises gasoline prices
FIREWORKS   MR. WAFFLE   AUNT M'S
take THIS EXIT
THIS IS IT!
THIS IS IT!

Increase your vocabulary
Say it with Flowers
Somebody's baby girl
clutches her ear and cries
in the back seat

RED DIRT   REAL FOOD   REAL FAST

South Carolina Welcome's You
blue snow on red clay mounds
The sun warms

                  RIDERS WEAR HELMETS
my shoulder
Night will bring
STARS
through my window to the East
before I reach Morgantown.

Folk Dancing
Dedicated to Beth Smith, 14 July 1998

Toe, Toe, Heel, Hop
Tricky little steps!

Move it along
Swing, Swing-

Give it your best shot
Quicken the pace-

Faster, Faster, FASTER
Frantic, hop step, step, STEP--

Toe, Toe, Step Toe, Toe
Step Toe, Step Toe, HOP

Criss-cross, Twirl about
Burst forth in laughter.

Fall back, trip me up
Trip, glide, move it in squares-

Emotions, Check your step
Jump and hop. Step.

Burst forth in laughter
and end with a SHOUT!

Kim Itoh and the Glorious Future

Kim Itoh
unpredictable
moves slowly on the darkened stage
in the slant of light
from left to right
his bare feet reaching
searching the uncharted
borderlands
of Butoh conversation

his arms lift up at right angles
shifting his graceful nude body
his swift hands cut upward
moving independently
like a ghost

this is the hellraiser
who has a reputation
to live up to-
this is the solo performer
angry and mildly
disturbing

did you come here
to be shocked
by the Glorious Future
of modern
Japanese
art?
a comically overtoned
glance?

Butoh - a dance in depth
Butoh – a dance of death

Dancing With No Intermission - Homage to Matsuko Tanaka

Heavenly Chickens
create their own works
full of poetic feeling
from the depths of sleep
eerie, otherworld
strong dancing to the theme
of night -
Nocturne.

Heavenly Chickens
dancing together
full of humor and pathos
strange radiance of life
the fantastical
rich body expressions
performed-
Nocturne.

Heavenly Chickens
legendary fame
becomes slowly visible
over two decades
no intermission
spectacular nature
a dream-
Nocturne.

Heavenly Chickens
unique character
critically acclaimed dancers
choreography
a narrative dream
slowly emerging sleep
deepens-
Nocturne.

*Matsuko Tanaka is considered the prima donna of Butoh, the Dance of
the Unmovables. Nocturne was created in 1995, an 80 minute
performance with no intermission. Ann Daly of the Village Voice,
November 19, 1996 wrote that it was "a thunderbolt from the gods."*

Köenigsee

On the passage from Köenigsee
swift winds bring low temperatures
clouds conceal marbled mountain peaks

Chiffon gray skies
press down on clustered red-tiled roofs,
Narrow doorways squeeze
slow moving tourists.

Long ferry boats glide silently
across the frigid green lake
laughing Germans sing of home
waves break beyond our boat.

In the final hour of night
before mountains disappear
my chilled body reaches downward
seeking shelter
in the next bus to Grödig.

Time to Draw

Time to draw:
Conversations and sounds
Machinery
Speaking in English
Tulip trees
Pines
Metal roofs
behind a row of houses-
1 blue-gray mountain
in the distance.

Time to draw:
1 that is finished
4 that are working
2 gray suede tennis shoes
2 blue and black sandals
2 beige leather wedgies
2 brown leather sandals

Time to draw:
Three pairs of denim jeans
1 pair of green jeans
1 pair of khaki slacks
a cough
a sniffle
sounds of pounding
on metal-

Time is up.

Analog Drawing

Use only a pencil
to write about
emotions contained
within your square.

Paint the picture
using lines
tag the image
with a word.

Write about
loneliness
make your anger
visible.

Keep looking
for an emotion
that bursts
off the page.

Subtle, jabbing
dispersing
the drawing will
tell it all.

Notes From an Exhibition at the Rupertinum - July 23, 1998

This female is asleep
Emilio Greco crosshatched her face
decisive and sensitive
pure contour in 1970.

Jean Dubuffet scribbled graffiti
wild lines - explosive
angry, black, fun in 1950
she fills the frame with her wide figure.

To the right of the page
Paul Klee masked his female figure
it was 1931 - she is tall and lean
as she faces to the right.

The Otto Meyer-Amden woman is still
she is gray, soft, and she lies in shadows
it is 1928 and the man is not yet fully awake
his round full muscles, swell as he writes.

Walking about

Turning

Two more drawings
contour male
lyrical female
Gerhard March's lines
go deeper still
the nude figure sits on the air

She turns her back to me
touches her knee
holds herself erect
I can never see through her eyes

her gaze is beyond my perception
I can never know her view in 1969.
I see him from behind
as he bends over, low
his dropped pants, ribs, and curved spine
arouse me as I linger behind him
out of his view.

Finally, a rounded knee
holds up his belly
lines sweep around and over

STOP!

begin again
just a bit of shade with a grey crayon
an abstract on yellowed paper
a loop to the right
a twirl down the center
a triangle in the corner
runs down to rest on top
of my thigh.

The lady with her mirror stretches
to touch her buttocks
against the bottom of the page
her feet cross and she pulls
inward to rest on her right arm
caressing her long hair
the mirror in her left hand
reflects her face
as she looks to see me
looking into her mirror
I see my own face
I long to see her face
but she turns toward the darkness
of the middle.

76

There was roundness and roundedness
in 1930
Andre Derain stroked the female
with choppy shadows of red pigment
neck & face
breasts & waist
abdomen & navel
arms & thighs
all red lines
on gray parchment paper
a classic pose
yet
the hand won't work.

Two lie side by side
on a bed facing me
their eyes are closed
he touches his feet
their strong, squat bodies
she reclines with her arms
above her head
reaching
broken in half
her body bright pink
drawn with black ink
surrounded by blue
that fades to green
their bed alive, glowing.

Should I stay here and wait
with Picasso, or
secretly leave this place?

Andre Masson has made
two drawings in 1944
he swings his arm into the air
presses black pigment into the paper

his strokes are long, sure
moving
moving
around and swirling
up and around
strong hands provide dark places
in which I come to enter
safe here, cool
this bower you have made for me
around the edges
on the side of your figures
my foot can be
firmly planted here
you have made a ground for me
to stand on
I find safety in your presence
I can see that you know the way.

Your face looks away from all viewers
as I touch the fur tips
I need to know for sure
a tuft on the forehead
shades your eyes
it's a hot July sun
that flashes on your navel
A sharp touch
to bristle the hand of any man
who dares to reach inside.

Here you are left exposed
a thistle of down there?
just at the knees?
a curved back from behind
an arm that broke off long ago

Your face looks away from me
there in the shade with only enough light
to form the fullness of your bottom lip

Forever you will remain encased
in the plastic box
and I turn to follow the woman
in the black dress
as she leaves the room.

The woman slightly smiles
as she looks to the ground
and here I have found you once again
in Salzburg!
William DeKooning
you are my first love
because darkness
left my soul in 1951.

I am here on the edge of the page
among the many lines
I struggled to find you
my pencil searching
sharply, deeply
your gestures are true
you stayed at your task
you worked to find
this man
I see in Salzburg today.

To Max

All is quiet tonight   Still
At the top of the hill   LIGHT
He wears a long dark hat   Bronze
Stands where the blue house lays   Spread
Heart an indentation   Shape
No arms and no muscles   Quiet
Only the green moon

    KNOWS

*Poem written after looking at two of Max Ernst's works
at the Haus der Kunst, Munich, Germany, July, 1999:*

*Young Man with Beating Heart (1944)
Petrified City (1935)*

In the Picasso Gallery

In the Picasso Gallery
a docent's voice warbles
about the Rose Period
and happier times.

Petrus Manach's name
written in black ink
like the first art patron.

It was a tough time
when he first saw El Greco's
monochromatic,
elongated figures.

He stands, hands on hips
in a white shirt with red tie
blue stripes slashed
across his forehead.

Step over here to view
a friend's suicide
from the early 1900's
in the Picasso Gallery.

Head of a Catalan Peasant
Homage to Joan Miro'

In the National Gallery
just beyond the Motherwell
is the yellow painting by Miro'.

Black and red circles
cover her outstretched hands
a blue star was blazoned
above her left shoulder
her wide face is red
her brown skirt dances.

A pale lady with yellow hair
looks across the golden room
she wears a soft yellow dress
her tan leather shoes
were woven in Paris.

This is the head
of a Catalan peasant.

A Moment of Calm
Homage to Max Ernst

A crooked blue sun
in a wide sky
tumbles
through blue, green, yellow
Impaled
on spiky green stems.

Blackbirds squat low
shout at the alligator
resting in the dark corner
watching for more
pinks and reds in the middle.

A lone dragonfly passes through
a painted arch
relaxing
a moment of calm.

The Grödig Stone

Deep ruby red wine
a color in shadow

The delicate flakes of metal flicker
like diamond dust in my drawer

The bottom is plain gray
flat indentations not easy to see

My finger rests on the subtle scar
a pointed oval shape

I am always a visitor
walking the familiar path of the village

The winding bicycle paths
surround the mountain peaks

In the crisp early morning light
a rainbow had enclosed the mountain

Even its memory has vanished
as I walk through fields of Queen Anne's Lace

In the twilight I look back to the village
the church steeple points to my return

Twilight will soon fall downward
cover the red tiled roof and marble staircase.

Memorial Day - A Sestina for Multiple Voices

In my mother's kitchen my aunts each begin to speak
about family achievements and God's great mercy.
They hover over the wooden table. They desire
hot casseroles wrapped in linen towels. With a spirit
of joy they cut into the fresh-baked apple pie. They sing
praises of children and pass new photos to show a truth.

One aunt conveyed a truth
not pleasing to speak
about recent news from Minnesota. Now she'll sing
praises about her daughter's life - speak of God's mercy.
My aunt's spirit
becomes confused like an old woman's diminished desire.

My daughter's love was my only desire
but I need to know the truth.
Tell me again of her spirit
dashed. I speak
about my daughter's life that is over. Mercy
is a dirge to sing.

Group your words into stanzas - make a poem sing
the indentation of lines can vary with desire
single words can occupy entire lines, like "mercy"
break up your words into the shape of truth
allow the shape to be the message you speak
unconventional punctuation is a path to the spirit.

The two women felt her spirit —
could they sing
in this cold place? They couldn't speak
of work, home, or desire
for clothing to hang in closets of truth
about unopened birthday cards filled with mercy.

My aunt holds an old photo and prays for mercy
she flicks away dust with a wipe of her shattered spirit
this year it's a more remote truth -
no picnics in my mother's kitchen. No voices to sing
around a wooden table. My mother's only desire
is for visitors who come to speak

You are proved right as you speak. Grant me a willing spirit.
Have mercy on me, O, God! Let my tongue sing
on Memorial Day. Let me desire innermost truth.

Slowly, Suddenly - Remembering Persephone

Summer afternoon
ripe for contemplation
the sun moves slowly
to center sky
stillness.

I remember
springtime
picking flowers
things happen suddenly.

I drifted in random circles
on the surface of quiet waters
beneath clustered branches.
The day can change suddenly
no movement in the tangled leaves
even birds seek shade today.

We danced through the wild flowers
suddenly
we were immovable
and grew old.

I shifted forward
undulating slowly
to an ancient rhythm
summer's sleep returned.

Random things bring quick changes
this evening is like
the moment before my birth

A full moon will rise this evening
soft gray shifts to deep indigo
my whole world spirals backwards
a storm changes my direction.

A scattering of stars
no clouds to hide them
I slip deep into placid dark waters
my body heals in the coldness.

Accidents occur suddenly
torn in half
I swim to the nether side
wait silently in darkness
my hands cut through the surface.

As you embrace me
the moon will bathe my body
winds blow my flesh dry

I am destined to live
in two world.

**In the Storms of April – Plunge
(A letter to December)**

We wait together beneath the surface
of frozen waters in February
dormant, settled, calm
we have already survived January

Of frozen waters in February
winter's sharp light sears the surface
we have already survived January
beneath heavy, urgent stillness

Winter's sharp light sears the surface
we begin to remember our faces
beneath heavy, urgent stillness
our names were carved in the ice

We begin to remember our faces
in the perfect snowfield of March
our names were carved in the ice
surrendering our identity to the sky

In the perfect snowfields of March
we lie prone, between vellum sheets
surrendering our identity to the sky
waiting to hold our ancient purpose

We lie prone, between vellum sheets
submerged dragonflies
waiting to hold our ancient purpose
beneath waters of shuffling script

Submerged dragonflies
forget the present happiness
beneath waters of shuffling script

89

anguish takes the future tense
Forget the present happiness
heavy rains in the depths of night
anguish takes the future tense
we are waiting to plunge deeper

Heavy rains in the depths of night
our bodies purged in forgetfulness
we are waiting to plunge deeper
when birds awaken us at dawn

Our bodies purged in forgetfulness
uneven breathing subsides
when birds awaken us at dawn
March is a dangerous month

Uneven breathing subsides
no distraction from the moment
March is a dangerous month
note it in our journal

No distraction from the moment
waiting beneath the surface
note it in our journal
slowly

Waiting beneath the surface
shooting stars breed disquiet
slowly
isolated inactivity becomes justified

Shooting stars breed disquiet
bursts of frenetic activity is noted
isolated inactivity becomes justified
pleasure is worth writing down

Our skins will shed in April
dormant, settled, calm
one final flight
we wait together beneath the surface.

Written in response to an essay by Jeff O'Brien.

Notes

Eluere, Christiane. *The Celts*. NY: Harry N. Abrams, Inc., 1993.

Kubler, George. *The Shape of Time.* New Haven and London: Yale University Press, 1962, p.79.

Palmer, Parker. *Let Your Life Speak, Listening for the Voice of Vocation. CA: Jossey-Bass Inc., 2000, p.54.*

Truiitt, Anne. *Daybook, The Journey of an Artist.* NY: Penguin Putnam, Inc. 1982, pp. 10-11.

Acknowledgments

Grateful acknowledgment is made to the editors of the following journals and anthologies in which these poems or earlier versions of them appeared.

In Other Words: "A Moment of Calm," "Sunday Morning in Winter";

Glory to God by Rita Choy-Ng: "A Mandate";

Taproot Literary Review: "A Place Unknown," "After an All-Night Rain: Remembering Dante," "Counting the Wounds," "Monday Afternoon Dessert";

Ginger Hill: "Counting the Wounds," "Dragon Fly";

Daily Athenian: "Even in Arcadia," "Three Acts";

Pro Christo A Journal of Ideas: "Surrounded";

From the Mountaintop: "Young Man with a Beating Heart";

Poetry's Elite: "Young Man with a Beating Heart."

About the Author

Photo by Suzy's Photo, Beaver Falls, PA

Lynda Lambert lives and works in the small village of Wurtemburg, located in the foothills of Western Pennsylvania. She is a graduate of Slippery Rock University of Pennsylvania and West Virginia University where she earned advanced degrees in Fine Arts and English. Currently she is Associate Professor of Fine Arts and Humanities at Geneva College in Beaver Falls, Pennsylvania where she teaches studio art, humanities, and contemporary poetry.

This book is her first published collection of poems. Here she develops her subject matter—nature, landscape, and journey. While her poems begin with keen descriptions of a place, she then moves the reader into a sense of mystery through her powerful reflections and insistent music. Always there is the notion of both a physical and spiritual journey – a pilgrimage.

About KotaPress

KotaPress, established by Hawk & Kara Jones in 1999, was started as a safe haven in which they could publish their own grief & healing artworks after the death of their son Dakota. Since its inception, KotaPress has extended this safe haven to other bereaved parents, artists, and poets around the world. KotaPress aims to continue offering a home for artworks created by artists who are on a healing path regardless of the tragedy that put them on the path in the first place.

www.KotaPress.com

Other Titles from KotaPress

A Different Kind of Parenting:
a print 'zine for parents whose children have died
ISSN1533-8886
Single issues $2.00
Subscription $8.00/year/4 issues

Flash Of Life, 2nd Edition
by Kara L.C. Jones
KotaPress, 2002
ISBN 1-929359-15-2
$15.00

Bone Marrow Boogie: The Dance of a Lifetime
By Janie Starr
KotaPress, 2002
ISBN 1-929359-16-0
$17.95

Colophon

Concerti: Psalms for the Pilgrimage, poems and reflections by Lynda Lambert, uses Times New Roman and Arial font sets.

The cover was designed by Hawk Jones.

Editor of this book was Kara C. Jones.

Manufacturing was by RPI.

Publisher of this book was Kota Press.

Special support for this book came from the following individuals and organizations:

Charles Robert (Bob) Lambert, my husband and fellow traveler in life who taught me how to dance with the wind.
Elizabeth Asche Douglas, my soul sister, for her encouragement to publish my first book.
Renae Applegate and Dawn Lindner, graduate students who read my first draft and and gave me their reflections on my poems.
My colleagues at Geneva College for their spiritual and professional guidance and personal friendship.
Geneva College for generous professional and financial support to spend each summer in Austria where I worked on completing the poems and drawings for this book.

To Sharon

Linda McKinney

Lambert · 2017